D060364&

Heinemann Library
Chicago, Illinois

Map Basics

Maxwell Baber

Designed by David Poole and Geoff Ward
Illustrations by International Mapping (www.internationalmapping.com)
Photo research by Alan Gottlieb and Tracy Cummins
Originated by Modern Age
Printed and bound in China by WKT

07 06 05
10 9 8 7 6 5 4 3 2 1

Library of Congress Cataloging-in-Publication Data
Baber, Maxwell.
  Map basics / Maxwell Baber.
     p. cm. -- (Map readers)
  Includes bibliographical references and index.
  ISBN 1-4034-6794-3 (hc) -- ISBN 1-4034-6801-X (pb)
  1. Map reading--Juvenile literature. 2. Maps--Juvenile literature. I. Title. II. Series.
  GA130.B13 2007
  912--dc22
                              2006003351

13 digit isbn hardback: 978-1-4034-6794-2
13 digit isbn paperback: 978-1-4034-6801-7

Acknowledgments
The author and publisher are grateful to the following for permission to reproduce copyright material
Alinari / Art Resource p. **7**; Biblioteca Marciana, Venice, Italy, Giraudon / Bridgeman
Art Library p. **6**; Digital Wisdom p. **4**; FAA courtesy Maptech p. **21**; George Diebold
Photography/ Iconica/ Getty Images p. **16**; NOAA courtesy Maptech pp. **5** (nautical chart),
20; Superstock p. **8**; ThinkStock/age footstock p. **27**; USGS p. **5** (courtesy Maptech), **22**, **23**
(courtesy Maptech); USGS National Center for Earth Resources Observation & Science p. **26**.

Cover map of Rocky Mountain National Park reproduced with permission of USGS courtesy Maptech

Compass image reproduced with permission of Silvia Bukovacc/Shutterstock.

Every effort has been made to contact copyright holders of any material reproduced in
this book. Any omissions will be rectified in subsequent printings if notice is given to the
publishers.

Special thanks to Daniel Block for his help in the production of this book.

The publishers and authors have done their best to ensure the accuracy and currency of all
the information in this book. However, they can accept no responsibility for any loss, injury,
or inconvenience sustained as a result of information or advice contained in the book.

Table of Contents

Some words are shown in bold, **like this**. You can find out what they mean by looking in the glossary.

Introduction

Have you ever traveled to a city or town outside of your neighborhood? Or visited relatives in another part of the country? If you answered "yes," a map most likely helped you get there.

A map is a picture of an area of the world that can have many practical uses. Transportation maps show roads, rivers, and cities to help people find their way around. Political maps show boundaries between countries. Topographic maps display the location of mountains and valleys. Weather maps show the average temperature, air pressure, or rainfall in a certain region.

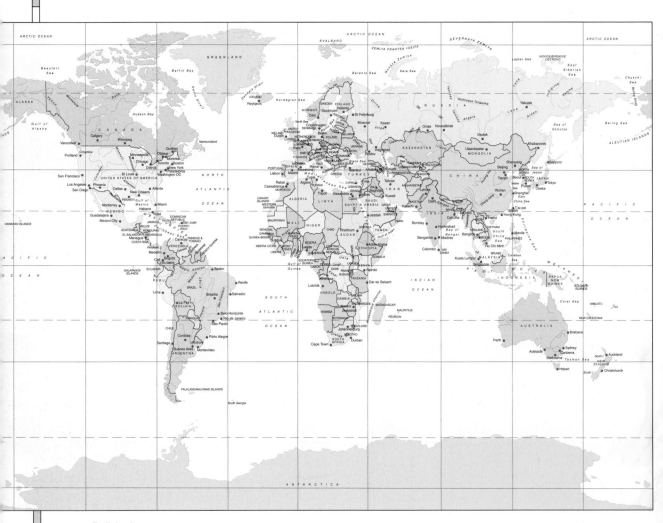

Political map.

Cartography, the study of maps, has never been more important than it is today. The world is changing rapidly, and computer mapping systems are now available to help us keep up with these changes. Modern transportation and communication systems have brought the entire world within our reach, and maps help us better understand this new global community.

By learning about different types of maps and understanding how to use and read them, we can explore the past and plan for the future. Get ready for an adventure: maps go everywhere!

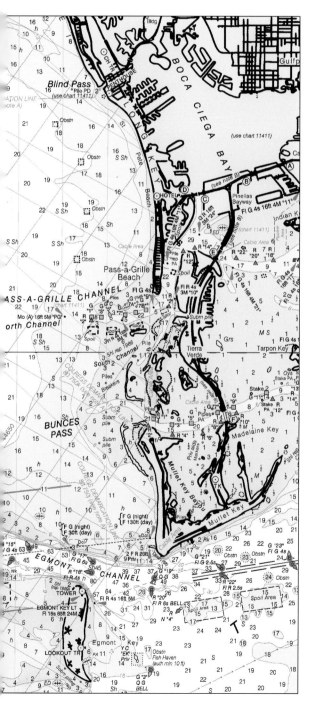

Nautical chart.

Topographic map.

The History of Mapping

Maps have been important tools since people first began to organize into civilizations. Prehistoric maps have been found on cave walls. Ancient clay tablets have also been discovered. These show where towns were located along rivers and between mountain ranges. The oldest map ever found dates back more than 4,000 years!

Scientific mapmaking was advanced by the ancient Greeks. They were the first to realize that the Earth is round, and they developed the system still used today for determining the location of any place in the world. The Greeks also calculated the Earth's size and shape, and defined the locations of the **equator** and poles. You will learn more about these features later.

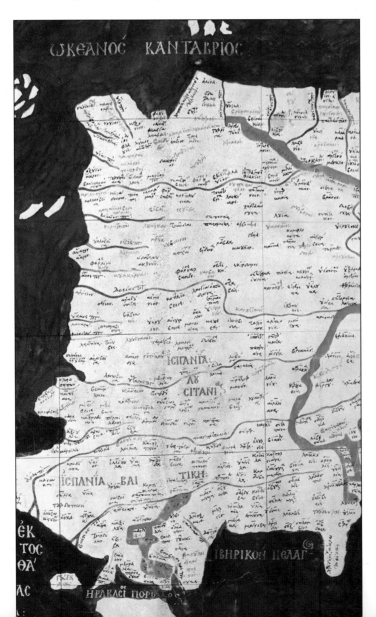

The most famous of the ancient Greek **geographers** was Claudius Ptolemy (AD 90–168), a scholar in Egypt who lived more than 18 centuries ago. Ptolemy produced an **atlas** that included information about the entire known world. An atlas is a bound collection of maps. Ptolemy's work later played an important role in the beginnings of global exploration.

This is a Medieval copy of a map of Spain and Portugal that Ptolemy created for his atlas.

In the 1300s, maps called portolan charts were created. These maps were amazingly accurate, and provided the first detailed coastline maps for navigating the seas around southern Europe. Many new maps were developed as explorers returned with information about previously unknown lands.

During the 1600s and 1700s, geographers made important advances in tools and techniques used to **survey** land. Land surveys require careful measurement of the locations of landscape features. By the late 1700s, cartographers completed the world's first national land survey in France.

Mapmakers today still use some of the methods created by our ancestors, but modern technologies have improved the accuracy of maps. Cameras mounted on airplanes take pictures for making maps of local landscapes. **Satellites** launched into space capture detailed images of the Earth's surface. These methods help us study our changing environment in more detail than ever before.

This is a portolan chart that shows the Black Sea and Eastern Mediterranean area including Greece and Turkey.

Getting to Know Your Globe

In order to understand maps, it is helpful to first become familiar with a globe. Globes are three-dimensional models of the Earth that are in the shape of a ball, or sphere.

If you look closely at a globe, you will see a line that that runs around the globe, called the equator. This line divides the Earth it into two equal half-spheres, or **hemispheres**. These two hemispheres are called the Northern Hemisphere (everything above the equator) and the Southern Hemisphere (everything below the equator).

Now look at the top of the globe. You should see a line that runs from the North Pole down to the South Pole, passing through the United Kingdom. This line is called the **Prime Meridian**. In 1884, an international treaty identified the Royal Observatory in Greenwich, England, as the location of the Prime Meridian.

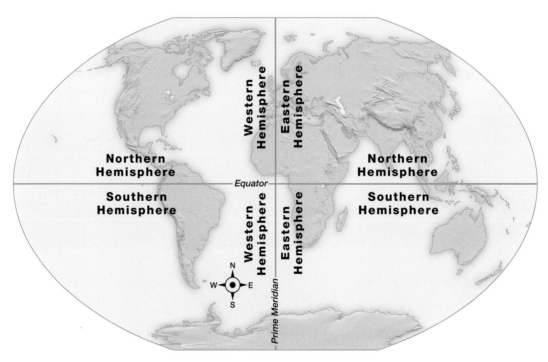

Together, the Prime Meridian and the equator divide the world into four sections: the Northern Hemisphere, the Southern Hemisphere, the Eastern Hemisphere, and the Western Hemisphere.

This map shows the location of the International Date Line.

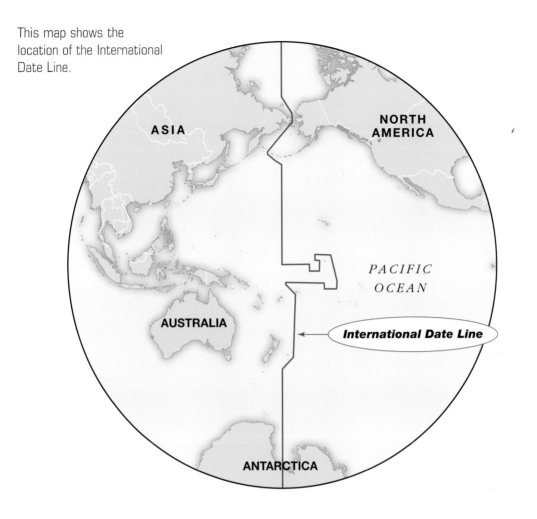

On the opposite side of the world from the Prime Meridian is the **International Date Line**. The date line runs through the middle of the Pacific Ocean. On the west side of the date line, it is one day later than on the east side. For example, if you cross the International Date Line going east toward North and South America, the day becomes one date earlier. If you cross this line going west toward Asia and Australia, the day becomes one day later.

It might seem strange that the date changes when you pass over a line, but the date line is needed because the Earth is round. Imagine you and a friend decide to leave your hometown and meet at the other side of the world. You go around the Earth toward the west. As you go, the hours get earlier. Your friend goes toward the east. The hours get later. When you finally meet, you would agree on the time, but your friend would think it is one day later than you do. We need the International Date Line to fix this problem.

Map Projections

Globes are very useful for getting a general picture of the Earth's features. However, the size and shape of globes make them impractical for most routine map uses, such as finding your way from place to place. A globe big enough to display city streets would be hundreds of feet tall! To make globes more useful, we transform them into maps. A map is a representation of selected features of the Earth on a flat surface. **Map projections** flatten the globe to create maps that can fit onto a textbook page or a computer screen.

Features on a globe have four characteristics: area, shape, distance, and direction. Mapmakers choose a type of map projection based on which of these characteristics is most important to the map's purpose. Map projections focus on only one of these characteristics, while the others are not accurate. These changes are called **distortions**. Some projections distort all four characteristics a little bit in order to limit the distortion of any one characteristic.

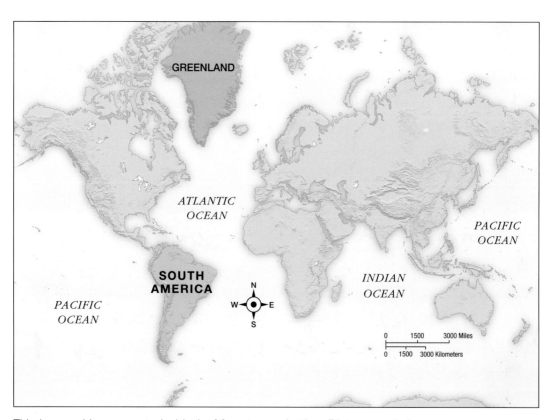

This is a world map created with the Mercator projection. Distance and size are not accurate on this type of projection.

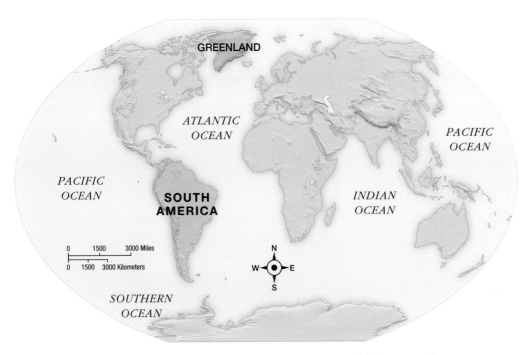

The Winkel Tripel projection shows size and distance on a map fairly accurately.

Some projections are designed for navigation. The Mercator projection was developed more than 400 years ago to help sailors find their way across oceans using only a **compass**. The Mercator projection is an excellent map for finding direction, but it distorts land areas near the North Pole and South Pole, making them look much bigger than they really are. This type of map projection would not be good to use if you wanted to get an accurate picture of the world.

Other map projections, such as the Winkel Tripel, represent the size of geographic features more accurately. This type of map projection can be used to compare population information in different parts of the world.

Examine the maps on these pages and notice the differences. Look at Greenland and compare its size with South America. Greenland is actually much smaller than South America, but you would never know that if you looked at a Mercator map. It is important to know the purpose of a map so you know which features are accurate.

Map Scale

A map is like a view from above. From a hot air balloon hundreds of feet above your community, you can easily recognize buildings, roads, parks, and trees. From an airplane window thousands of feet above the ground, you can see cities, highways, forests, lakes, and mountain ranges. Seeing the world from different heights is like making maps at different scales.

Map scale tells you how much the real world has been reduced in size in order to fit it onto a piece of paper or computer screen. The **scale bar** on a map tells how many real miles are represented by every inch (or centimeter) on the map. It helps you figure out the distance between places.

This is a large-scale map of New York state.

Map scale varies depending upon the amount of area shown on a map. Most maps do not show the entire planet. **Large-scale** maps provide a lot of detail about a local area. For example, city maps show the locations of streets, buildings, and parks, and are considered large scale. **Small-scale** maps provide much less detail about broader areas. World maps showing the locations of nations and oceans are small scale. Large- and small-scale maps can represent different-sized areas on the same size piece of paper.

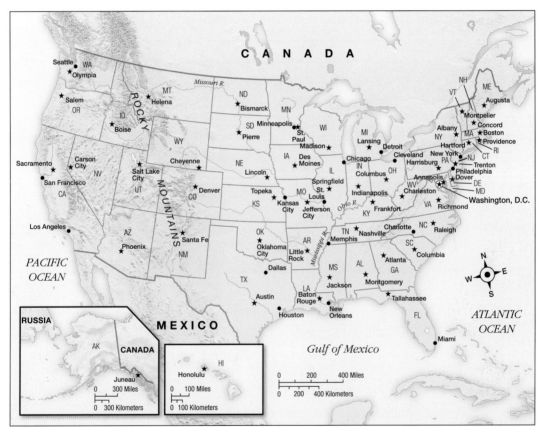

This is a small-scale map of the United States.

Compare the map of the United States with the map of New York on these pages. Both of these maps have scale bars. The scale bars provide information about the distances across each map. Try stretching a piece of string between two locations, and then compare this length with the scale bar to estimate distance. The map of New York state is at a larger scale than the map of the United States. A map of New York city would be at an even larger scale.

The Elements of a Map

In order to use a map, you need to know the map's purpose. The **map title** will tell you what kind of information you will find on the map. You also need to know what types of features are included on your map. Think of all the things you can see when you look out your window. There may be trees, playgrounds, sidewalks, homes, streetlights, or public parks. When you think about it, there are lots of things that you might include on a map. However, if you were to include too many features, the map would be very difficult to read. A mapmaker must show only the features that are important for the type of map he or she is creating.

The first things you should look for on a map are the map title and key. They tell you what kind of information is on the map and what the symbols mean.

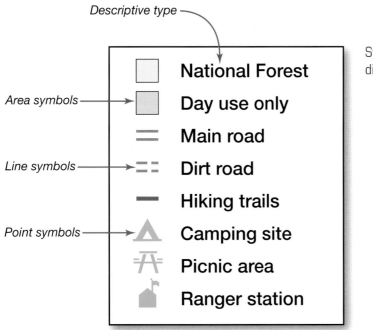

Descriptive type —

National Forest

Area symbols ——→ Day use only

Main road

Line symbols ——→ Dirt road

Hiking trails

Point symbols ——→ Camping site

Picnic area

Ranger station

Symbols on a map key can differ from map to map.

Features on a map are represented by symbols. The use of symbols saves space on a map and allows more features to be shown. Symbols also make maps easier to read. But how do you know what each symbol means? Mapmakers include a **map key** (or map legend) to explain the symbols. A key shows each symbol and describes what each one represents.

Points, lines, and areas are the three basic types of symbols used on maps. Point symbols show you where specific things are located, such as a museum or park. Point symbols are sometimes shown with squares, circles, stars, or triangles. Capital cities are often represented with stars. Sometimes mapmakers use point symbols that look like the features they represent. For example, a church is often represented by a symbol that looks like a small building with a cross on top.

Line symbols are used to represent things that are long but not wide, like roads and bike paths. A single line is typically used to show where a neighborhood road is located, and a double line often symbolizes an interstate highway.

Area symbols are used to represent features that are both long and wide, such as countries, oceans, forests, and parks. These are shown by either marking their borders or through a special color or pattern. For example, a forest is often shown in green. An ocean or lake is often shown in blue.

Finding Direction

Imagine that you are on a camping trip. You have been walking in the woods for hours, and you notice that your counselors are starting to look nervous. You hear one of them say, "we should have gotten there by now." Then one of them asks if anyone has a compass, and your counselor pulls out a small circular object. She takes a hard look at it, and begins to point in one direction. Suddenly you start walking again, and pretty soon you are back at the parking lot where your trip began.

Figuring out which direction you are heading can be very important when you are trying to find your way in an unfamiliar place. Fortunately, there are tools that help us find direction. North, south, east, and west are the four main directions, and are commonly called the **cardinal directions**.

Many people use a compass to find directions. A compass uses a magnetic needle that always points toward the north. A magnet is a metal object with properties that cause it to attract to other magnetic objects. Magnets are useful for finding direction because the Earth has magnetic properties. Magnetic compasses have been used for navigation for more than 500 years!

The directions in between the cardinal directions are called the intermediate directions. These include northwest (nw), northeast (ne), southwest (sw), and southeast (se).

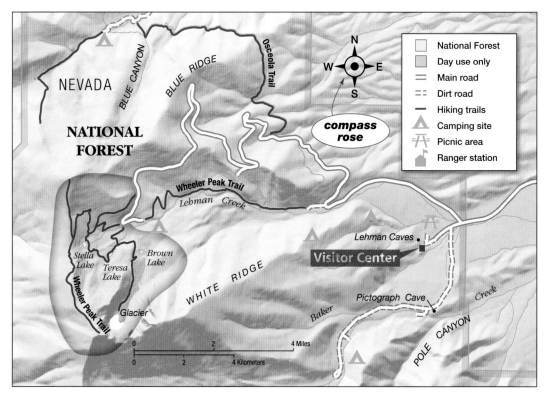

You must first know what direction your map is facing before you can use it properly. Look for the compass rose to get you started.

The face of a compass is called a **compass rose**. When the magnetic needle is pointing north, you can use the compass rose to identify the cardinal directions. This can be very useful at night or during cloudy days when the Sun is hidden from view.

As you know, maps are also important tools that help us find our way. While compasses tell which way we are heading, maps help us choose the best route to get somewhere. But how do you find directions on a map? Most maps have a small symbol, also called a compass rose, that shows you the directions on a map. If you know how to use a map and a compass together, you will be able to find your way in almost any situation.

Finding a Location

Most of us use maps in everyday situations, such as finding a store in a new part of town. In these kinds of situations, we just need to know which direction we should head toward, what street to turn onto, or which bus to take to get there. But what if you wanted to know the *exact* location of a place?

Maps and globes use a system called the **geographic grid** to provide an address for any location in the world. The geographic grid uses imaginary lines to identify location in two parts. The first part is called **latitude**, which measures north-south location. The second part is called **longitude**, which measures east-west location. Lines of latitude and longitude form a grid that looks like a big net thrown across the globe. Each line of latitude and longitude has its own number, called a **degree** (written as the symbol °). Together, these two numbers pinpoint an exact location.

The most significant latitude is the equator, an imaginary line found halfway between the North Pole and the South Pole. The equator is defined as 0 degrees latitude, because this is where the measurement of latitude begins. Other significant latitudes are the poles. The North Pole is 90 degrees North. The South Pole is 90 degrees South.

The most significant line of longitude is the Prime Meridian, which runs from the North Pole to the South Pole. It is defined as 0 degrees longitude because it is where the measurement of longitude begins.

In order to identify a location, we also have to determine two more things. First, is the location north or south of the equator? Second, is it east or west of the Prime Meridian? Let's look at New York City as an example. New York City has a latitude of 41 and is north of the equator, so we would write this as 41° N. Now let's find its longitude. New York City has a longitude of 74 and is west of the Prime Meridian, so we would write this as 74° W. Together, New York City's location is written as 41° N 74° W.

While it may seem complicated, the geographic grid system is an excellent way to locate any place on Earth. For centuries, explorers and other travelers have used this system to find safe passageways through rough waters, locate a new area of land, or to find their way home. Explorers and seafarers today still use this system to find their way around the world.

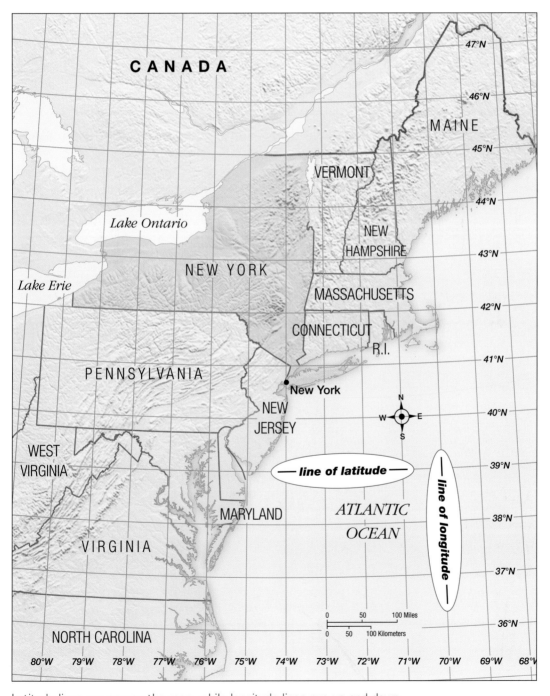

Latitude lines run across the map, while longitude lines run up and down.

Types of Maps

Now that you know how to read a map, you can explore the different ways we use maps. The type of map you need depends on the kind of information you are seeking.

Reference Maps

There are many different types of maps, but reference maps are the kind you are most likely to use. Reference maps provide general information that is useful for many purposes, including navigation. Airplane pilots and sailors use special types of reference maps called charts. Whether at sea or in the air, these charts are used to determine location and plot routes. Another type of reference map is a political map, which shows the boundaries between states or countries. A type of reference map you might use often is a road map.

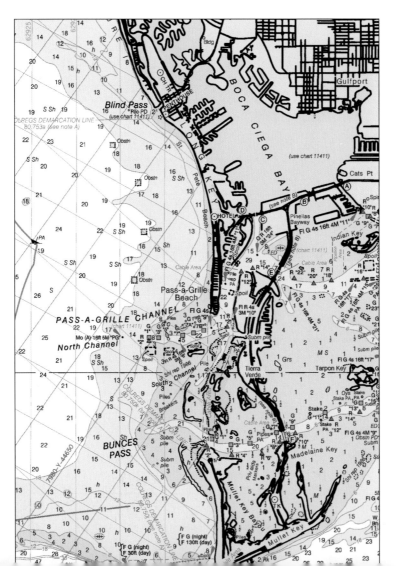

Sailors navigate different types of waterways. Safe navigation requires accurate information about water depth, underwater hazards, shoreline landmarks, and navigational aids such as buoys and lighthouses.

Harbor charts such as this one help sailors navigate areas near land that may have many hazards, such as sandbars or rocks.

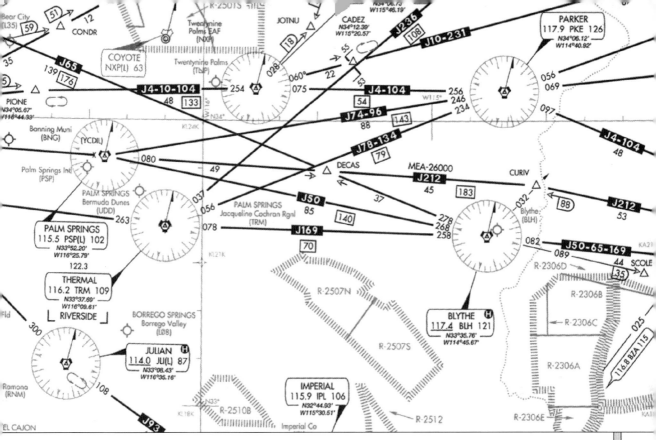

Aeronautical charts show the highways of the sky. The black lines indicate the different routes pilots can take.

Nautical charts produced in the United States include harbor charts, coastal charts, general charts, and sailing charts.

Airplane pilots need maps to help them navigate from airport to airport. Airplanes move through the sky much faster than ships travel through water, so pilots must make navigational decisions much more quickly than sailors. Different kinds of **aeronautical charts** are produced to help airplane pilots find their way.

Commercial airlines transport millions of passengers each year from city to city. Their aircrafts are equipped with the latest technologies to help pilots fly safely from place to place. Pilots use computerized mapping systems to guide their flights. They also get direction from controllers on the ground. These controllers use **radar** systems to keep track of many airplanes at once.

Pilots of small private planes usually navigate based on landmarks they can see on the ground. Aeronautical charts used for general aviation needs are designed to include cities, highways, railroads, airports, and other visible landmarks. These charts also include information about **restricted** areas and controlled airspace where private planes are not allowed to fly.

This shaded relief map shows the mountain ranges of North America.

While some reference maps help us find our way, others communicate information about the Earth's features. Every location on Earth has an **elevation**, which is the measure of its height above or below sea level. The difference between higher and lower elevations on a map is called relief.

The Earth's physical landscape is also known as its terrain. Showing the features of terrain on a map is a big challenge for cartographers (mapmakers). Maps are flat, but mountains and valleys are three-dimensional features. Cartographers use two methods for showing terrain's three dimensions.

Some maps represent mountains and hills with symbols that look like mountains as viewed from the side. In recent years, this artistic approach has included a more realistic-looking process called shaded relief. **Shaded relief maps** look like the sun shining across the landscape, leaving shadows to one side of hills and mountains.

More scientific symbolization of terrain is used in **topographic maps**. These maps represent the different elevations of the Earth's terrain with **contour lines**. Each contour line represents one elevation all along the length of the line. To measure the steepness of a hill, compare the distance between two contour lines. Lines that are close to each other represent steeper land. Lines that are farther apart represent land that is fairly flat.

On contour maps, the closer the lines are to each other, the steeper the slope.

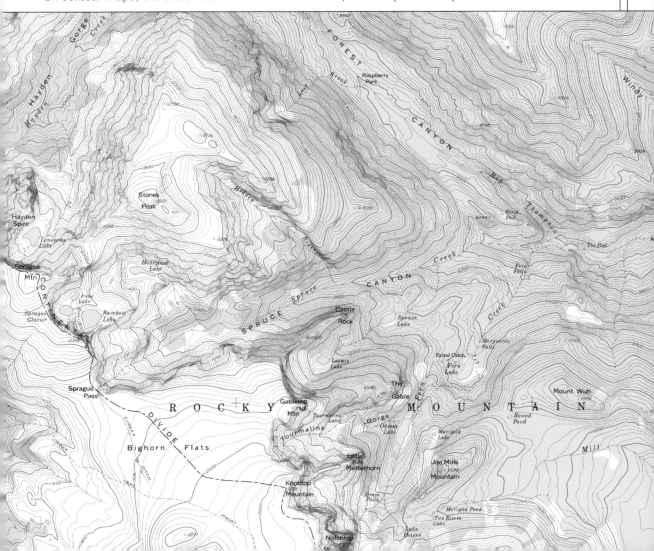

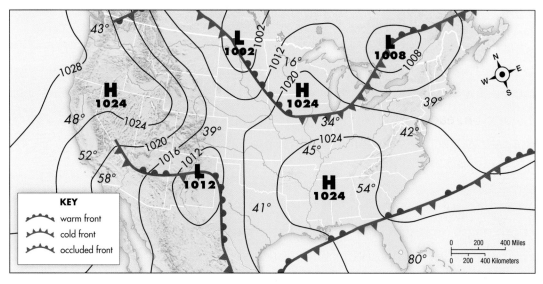

Weather maps are just one of many different thematic maps.

Thematic Maps

Reference maps show a lot of different geographic features. Thematic maps, on the other hand, focus on a single feature. They can help us understand characteristics of a region or compare things around the world. There are many different types of thematic maps. Some show the types of soil or vegetation growing in a particular area. Others communicate information about human population or agricultural production.

Thematic maps are being used more and more to help us make sense of the world. Because of computers, they are also now much easier to make. Weather maps are good examples of thematic maps in action. Some weather maps show the paths of storms and other types of weather. Others show the temperature across a country. You can recognize these as thematic maps because they focus on one characteristic (such as temperature or rainfall) at a time.

Thematic maps can represent amounts of something across broader locations like states or nations. These maps use shaded colors to represent higher and lower numbers. Darker colors usually represent higher values and lighter colors represent lower values. Some of these maps use numbers that have been collected for places like counties, states, or nations. This method is often used for mapping information about people and their activities. **Population density**—the number of people living in a certain area—is commonly mapped using this method.

Some thematic maps use dots to represent the number of something found in a location, such as population density. Rather than using one dot per person, each dot usually represents a certain number of people so that the map is readable. For example, pretend you wanted to represent the population of a large city. There might be more than one million people living in that city. That many dots would make the map very hard to read. By increasing the number of people represented by each dot, the map will be easier to read.

Thematic maps can also use the size of symbols like circles or squares to represent the number of something found in a location. The more of something there is, the larger the symbol will be. Think again about mapping population. This kind of thematic map would be a good choice if you wanted to compare the locations of large cities in the United States. The symbol representing each city will be sized according to population value, making it easy to see where cities with the most people are located.

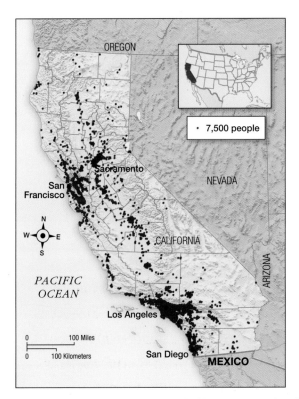 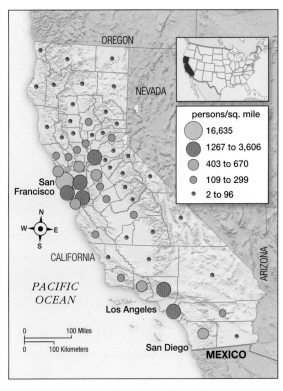

Above is a dot density map (left) and proportional symbol map (right) showing California's population by county. Even though the maps display the same type of information, they look very different.

The Future of Mapping

Not long ago, maps were drawn by hand. People who wanted to use maps had to find printed copies. But modern technologies have changed the way maps are made and used.

Computers are responsible for the biggest changes in mapmaking and map use. Computerized maps can be carried anywhere and provide more information than ever before. A technology called Geographic Information Systems (GIS) makes it possible to link computerized maps with electronic databases. These databases are like large warehouses of digital information.

Satellite photographs look like very detailed maps.

Geographic Information Systems have many uses. Businesses use them to identify where their customers are from to help them find the best locations for new offices and shops. Governments may use these "smart maps" to manage cities, states, and regions. Airplanes mounted with special cameras produce photographs that can be used in a Geographic Information System. For example, cities and counties use these photos to keep up with changes such as the development of new neighborhoods.

Satellites take even more detailed pictures. For example, satellite imagery can record the amount of heat energy released by objects on the ground. Farmers can use these kinds of pictures to identify areas where their crops might need extra attention.

Satellites are also used to help us find our way. Global Positioning System (GPS) satellites can identify our location and the direction in which we are traveling. Some cars have GPS displays that help drivers find their way from place to place.

Modern mapping tools like these put the world at our fingertips and give us a better picture of our global community. With the rise of computers, cartography continues to grow as an exciting professional field. Maps play an important role in our lives as they help us keep up with our changing world.

GPS devices can be small enough to take with you anywhere.

Make Your Own Maps

Now that you understand the basics of mapping, you can begin working with maps. Here are a few activities you can try.

1. **Make a map of your classroom.**
   a. Take a blank sheet of paper and draw an outline of your classroom.
   b. Draw symbols representing doors and windows.
   c. Draw a symbol representing the teacher's desk.
   d. Draw symbols representing students' desks.
   e. Draw symbols representing book shelves.
   f. Draw symbols representing other features of your classroom.
   g. Label all of the features you have drawn on your map in a map key.
   h. Use a compass and draw a compass rose showing the cardinal directions.
   i. Give your map a title.

2. **Make a map of your school.**
   a. Take a blank sheet of paper and draw an outline of your school grounds.
   b. Sketch an outline of your school buildings.
   c. Label a variety of school features such as a playground, athletic field, library, cafeteria, auditorium, your classroom, and the school office.
   d. Use a compass and draw a compass rose showing the cardinal directions.
   e. Give your map a title.

3. **Create a map of an imaginary country.**
   a. Use a variety of color pencils or markers to shade in the country and its borders with other countries.
   b. Color the oceans and seas.
   c. Create a map legend with point, line, and area symbols. Include a scale bar.
   d. Label the oceans.
   e. Draw a compass rose showing the four cardinal directions.
   f. Give your map a title.

Maps can also help you learn the names of states, countries, and continents. Make a copy of this map and try filling out the names of the U.S. states. You can fill in each state with a different color to show the borders.

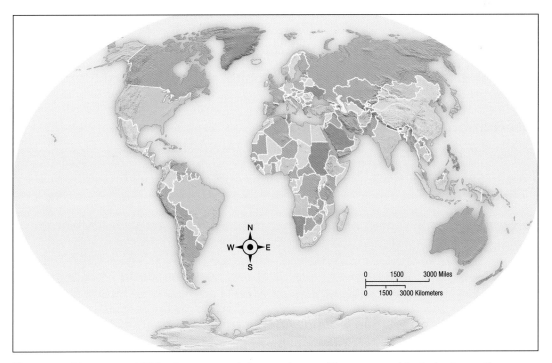

Now copy this map and fill in the names of the continents. You may need to look at an atlas or a globe to help you.

Glossary

aeronautical chart chart that pilots use to navigate the skies

atlas bound collection of maps

cardinal direction one of the four main directions including north, south, east, and west

cartography study of maps. A person who makes maps is called a cartographer.

compass tool used to help find direction

compass rose the face of a compass. Also the symbol on a map that indicates the cardinal directions

contour line line on a map connecting points of a land surface that are the same elevation

degree unit of latitude or longitude used to locate places on Earth

distortion feature of a map that is not accurate

elevation height of the land in relation to sea level

equator imaginary line that divides the Earth into the Northern and Southern Hemispheres; it is the same distance from the North and South Poles

geographer person who studies the Earth's physical features

geographic grid system that divides a map into smaller squares using horizontal and vertical lines so you can find places more easily

hemisphere one half of the Earth. Hemispheres are measured from north or south of the equator or west or east of the Prime Meridian.

International Date Line imaginary line on a globe that separates the calendar days between the Eastern and Western Hemispheres

large-scale map map that shows a fairly small area, on which details are relatively large

latitude lines on a map or globe that run east and west; lines of latitude are also called parallels

longitude lines on a map or globe that run north or south; lines of longitude are also called meridians

map key also called map legend. A table that shows and explains all symbols, lines, and colors used on the map.

map projection way of representing the round surface of the Earth on a flat surface

map scale amount that a map has been reduced from the size of the real place

map title feature on a map that identifies the content of the map

nautical chart map that sailors use to find their way at sea

population density number of people living in a certain area

Prime Meridian 0° longitude meridian; all other longitudes are measured from the Prime Meridian

radar device that helps locate and track distant objects

restricted intended only for people who have permission

satellite object put into orbit around Earth that sends back scientific data

scale bar feature on a map that tells you the relationship between a distance on the map and the distance in the real world

shaded relief map map that shows differences in land height with shading

small-scale map map that shows a large area, on which individual details are relatively small

survey detailed map of an area of land

topographic map map that shows differences in land height

Further Reading

Beasant, Pam. *How to Draw Maps and Charts.*
  Tulsa: E.D.C. Publishing, 1993.

Bredeson, Carmen. *Looking at Maps and Globes.*
  New York: Children's Press, 2002.

Stefoff, Rebecca. *The Young Oxford Companion to Maps and Mapmaking.*
  New York: Oxford University Press, 1995.

Wade, Mary Dodson. *Types of Maps.*
  New York: Children's Press, 2003.

Index

*Italicized numbers indicate
illustrations, photographs,
or maps.*